The Female Image of God

Dave Deal

ROYSTON
Publishing

BK Royston Publishing
P. O. Box 4321
Jeffersonville, IN 47131
502-802-5385
http://www.bkroystonpublishing.com
bkroystonpublishing@gmail.com

© Copyright – 2021

All Rights Reserved. No part of this book may be reproduced, stored in a retrieval system, or transmitted by any means without the written permission of the author.

Cover Design: Elite Book Covers

ISBN-13: 978-1-955063-06-7

King James Version Scriptural Text – Public Domain

New King James Version (NKJV) - Scripture taken from the New King James Version®. Copyright © 1982 by Thomas Nelson. Used by permission. All rights reserved.

NHEB –

Printed in the United States of America

Dedication

In honor of my mother, Margaretta Deal: this book has a lot to do with her guidance and protection during my childhood years. At the age of three years, I had a series of nightmares, of being chased by a being appearing like a shadow, not having any features except the form of a man. I was a sleepwalker, and walking in my sleep down 13 steps. I heard my mother say, "Get that girl a bottle," who is my younger sister two years younger than I. In my sleep or dreaming, I turned around to see this being with my sister's bottle and his finger on the tip of the nipple. I decided I would get it from him, and as I went up the stairs, I got bigger and as I got closer, the shadow started coming down toward me with a knife. So I turned to run through the living room to the kitchen where my mother was. As I told her the bogeyman was trying to kill me, she said, "It's a dream, it's a dream." I knew she didn't believe me, but it was real to me. But the dreams kept happening, the same thing over and over, I was being chased by this being. The being would change form, but had a weapon and would chase me until I woke up from sleep to crawl in at the foot of the bed with my mother and father. I could hear my father say, "'You've got to do something about that boy." Well, my mother read me the Bible, the big white book, that had the gold letters that read "The Living Word." She showed me pictures of God, in creation, in black and white, my first introduction to God. The last time this shadow chased me as I ran down the steps, my mother was sitting in a chair by the front door. As I saw her, I ran toward her as this being followed with a blade in his hand. My mother stood up and wrestled with it until he dropped the knife and disappeared. As I came more into the knowledge of God, I always wondered how my mother entered into my dream. I found the answer. The power of a praying mother causes her presence to protect her children from any evil presence. My mother is a woman of life. I came to realize God deals with some through their parents. My father, as I knew him was quiet and didn't speak much; my mother kept us together by playing cards or games, to see how we functioned with each other. I found God in Romans 12:3 that God has dealt to every man the measure of Faith, and it was like my mother, who also worked puzzles, those thousand pieces, or in the newspaper. She could take words and unscramble them and make them work. The female side of God operates by using words to work for her. We must pay attention to our parents because some of God's ways are in them. He's teaching us great lessons through them. One commandment with promise, "Honor thy father and thy mother that thy days may be long upon the land, which the Lord thy God giveth thee." Exodus 20:12 (KJV)

Acknowledgements

My father in the ministry, Bishop William C. Latta, who helped me to believe the bible way of doing things by the book and created an atmosphere where God could move with freedom.

Special thanks to Pastor Derrick and Clarissa Wilson, and Pastor Ray and Erma Thomas, for developing my teaching gift.

To my Pastor, Dr. F. Bruce Williams, who gives out keys to every member, saying you read too fast.

Table of Contents

Dedication	iii
Acknowledgements	vii
Introduction	xi
Chapter 1	1
The Female Image of God	
Chapter 2	5
The Creation	
Chapter 3	11
The Birth Order	
Chapter 4	15
Eve's Decisions	
Chapter 5	21
Women of Life	
Chapter 6	27
Two Kinds of Women	

Chapter 7	39
Taught Wisdom	
Chapter 8	43
Wisdom is a Female Person	
Chapter 9	55
Wisdoms Identity	
Chapter 10	59
Jesus brings Wisdom	
Chapter 11	69
Paul's Teaching	
Chapter 12	77
Two Wisdoms	
Chapter 13	81
John's Revelation	

Introduction

This knowledge is nothing new to scholars, ministers, and intellectuals. They have been discussing this issue for centuries. It appears very few of them do study their Bibles or ask the Father in prayer about who He is. This is how I discovered that the Father answers those who ask Him questions according to what's written in his Word. The Gender of God is what He says it is, not what we determine, or think He ought to be. When women and men discuss the image of God, they must tune in to his language, and learn the way He divides, adds, and multiplies. If only we would listen more. God gave us parents so we would experience both genders, and how we should relate to them. They are different in form, personality, and spirit. The Father is more authoritative and protective and the mother is gentle and caring. These features of God are to show us His complete and perfect balance in one being.

The power to produce a perfect Son, Jesus, who has both genders in him, to continue the same image in all of us. Male and female, in the image of God. Jesus said the Holy Spirit would teach us the truth, or God's language. The words of God are pure, not like men, which are mixed and deceitful. One must become a child and humble ourselves, not to know anything then we can sit in the elementary class with the teacher, the Holy Spirit and learn about the heavenly family. We should not allow men or women to tell us about our Father's gender and why He's plural. All scripture is from the KJV and the New KJV.

Chapter 1

The Female Image of God

The nature of God is still the most mysterious quest to be explored: This Being that most of us believe exists and exercise our faith in His power to give life to every creature and creation in our universe. But to study the gender of this Being is an incredible journey, that He himself lays out for us to learn. Until we study the divine nature of God, we are lost. Even though we have come into great knowledge, mankind is still learning. We must return to the beginning of creation to find what caused the problems between God and man, men and women, and the children. The mystery of the woman is one key we must not overlook. In the first book of the Bible, called Genesis, we find God introducing Himself, since no one else can do it better. It states in Genesis Chapter 1, Verse 27, "So God created man in his own image, in the image of God created he him; male and female created he them" (KJV). Upon reading this passage, we learn that God is telling us how we were created in His image, and it reflects on His plural nature. God is male and female, and mathematically He gives us the ratio of being twice as much male than He is female, for the female is male also. But to explore the female side of God is almost untouched and explained enough for us to relate to Him in a perfect balance. God Himself asks us to seek, search, and learn of Him, so we can understand Him as a person, with a personality, and character, to learn how to live with Him in His world. The world of God is the place to begin. If one tries to find Him in this world, it can be difficult, because He is invisible to the senses of every human being. The book we call the Bible is where we begin to read about Him, and to study His nature. He stated in Genesis, that He's male and female. Of every species on the planet there is male and female, even the trees are called male, Genesis 1:11b: "and the fruit tree yielding fruit after his kind" (KJV). The female is hidden in the trees and plants, and we know by the offspring they produce, called "fruit." Why? Because when God speaks, He directs His male and female seed into the ground and the plant kingdom begins to reproduce after their kind, as it is written: The Lord God made us after His kind, male and female. But it's the female image of God that's the focus here.

Chapter 2

The Creation

When God created Adam, He created him plural, like Himself, but the female image is hidden in Adam, the same as God Himself. God the father carries within Himself the chromosomes of male and female genes and gave to Adam to have the same genes within himself. To understand the powerful nature of God, we must take thought of how He brought forth the first man. In Genesis 2:7, it says, "And the Lord God formed the man from the dust of the ground and breathed into his nostrils the breath of life; and man became a living soul" (KJV). The Almighty God of the universe was on the ground on his knees, while Adam was lying lifeless when He breathed His breath of eternal life, or spirit of life, into Adam, and filled up his whole being. Then God gave Adam dominion over the cattle and the fish of the sea, and creeping things and over the whole earth. After He gave Adam the commandment to eat of every tree in the garden except the tree of the knowledge of good and evil. He gave to Adam a woman, who is a weapon, to help him keep that dominion over all His creation. The female image of God is a hidden weapon that God kept secret from eternity past, and not one angelic being knew he was male and female, and only learned of his plural nature during creation. Adam confirmed that God is male and female. In Genesis 2:24:

"Therefore shall a man leave his father and his mother and shall cleave unto his wife: and they shall be one flesh" (KJV). Adam called God his father and mother; this plural nature of God is what makes Him perfect and able to create species apart to come together and reproduce. When He brought forth the woman from Adam's rib, He was expressing His love nature in the opposite form. This love nature of God in them would rule all creation with obedience and authority. But Adam made two mistakes: he didn't ask God for his name, nor a name for his wife. In relating to the Almighty God, the lesson Adam taught us was one must ask God questions about anything if you need an answer. But Adam thought the name "woman" was sufficient and didn't ask God any questions about her. One lesson I learned is don't suppose you know everything, because if you don't ask the Almighty, He won't tell you. The woman needed a name for herself to be able to live up to the meaning and power of the female image of God and be able to operate in it. I understood Adam's mistake, that most of us husbands make, not asking God the name of your wife. Your wife has a personal name that only God knows, and if you don't ask Him, it may be the cause of your fall. When the Lord God said, "Let us make man in our image," there was a female in the meeting. He's talking to His creative beings in the plan of creating mankind, the female image of God was part of the creation of man and woman with God. In the natural, when a man and woman come together to be one, they are operating in the image of God to create another being, so it was with God's plan in creation, to continue His vision to populate the entire planet. The female image was created to operate with the male image of God to subdue and rule the earth. A husband must know the name and nature of his wife so they can become one and grow together in the grace of life that this creative genius would be displayed in both sexes and would show the diversity of the manifold wisdom of God.

Chapter 3

The Birth Order

It all began when the Lord birthed Adam out of His love for a family to dwell on the earth, and to live with them. When God caused a deep sleep to fall upon Adam, He again was on his knees to do surgery on Adam and He took one of his ribs, and made he a woman. He instead did a cesarean side section because of His ability to cause man to birth the woman, so that Adam would love her. And He closed up the flesh of Adam, so the open womb would not be seen. Because the woman was now brought forth, God moved the womb to the center of the woman, so He could form the fetus in the belly and bring forth the child from the womb. In Jeremiah 1:5 "Before I formed thee in the belly, I knew thee; and before thou came forth out of the womb, I sanctified thee, and I ordained thee a prophet unto the nations." Adam and the woman were not born physically like the rest of mankind, they were created. God is intelligently creative, and is there anything too hard for the Lord? The second order of God is when men sin or make mistakes. He washes us from our sins. So He commands husbands to wash their wives with the washing of water by His Word, or speaking life to her with God's Word Ephesians 5:26. The women would birth and wash their babies to clean them. This is Love's way. In the book of John 4:10, "Herein is love, not that we loved God, but that he loved us."

Man does not love God first, God birthed him. So God loves man and causes man to birth his wife so he would love her. The woman would love their children whom they birth, this is the order of God. If a man and woman would remain in the image of God, they would become fruitful as the Lord God had said they would. But something happened. When Eve disobeyed God and her husband and listened to the serpent instead of what God said, she ate from the tree of the knowledge of good and evil and gave it to her husband and he did eat. Eve desired independence from God and her husband, and to be her own god and stand on her own. But the image of God doesn't function independently. It operates in unity to keep proper order and rank. Our desire to do our own will and be independent is contrary to the way the Godhead intended mankind to live. When the Lord God set judgement upon Adam and his wife, and not a curse, He only cursed the ground for Adam's disobedience. Adam would have to till the ground, work harder and eat bread from the sweat of his brow. But God gave him seed, as he drove him out of the garden. But to the woman, he added more suffering in childbirth. So that the woman would love her children, more than her own personal desires. It may appear a severe judgement the Lord put upon Eve, but the woman was given strength to pass through death to bring forth life. This power over death was given to women in childbearing. Men die in giving birth, as God put Adam in a deep sleep, to show that men cannot enter through that kind of pain and be awake.

Chapter 4

Eve's Decisions

Genesis 3:20 says, "And Adam called his wife's name Eve; because she was the mother of all living" (KJV). This is the first time the woman was given a name and identity; now Eve could live up to her name, and tend to all the life that needed her help outside the garden. In Genesis 4:1-2, it says, "And Adam knew Eve his wife; and she conceived, and bare Cain, and said, I have gotten a man from the Lord. And she again bare his brother Abel. And Abel was a keeper of sheep, but Cain was a tiller of the ground." We read Cain tilling the ground like Adam but Abel was keeping the sheep. Who taught Abel? His mother, who also became the first Shepherd and trained Abel. But there are only two children; and Adam and Eve had a command to be fruitful and multiply and replenish the earth. Like most marriages, there are disputes, and who wins, the woman. So the absence of other children is apparent. And how old were Cain and Abel? What age were they when they began to work with their parents? That's how long there was no intimacy between Adam and Eve. In most situations, if someone or thing (the serpent) is talking to your wife, in a disrespectful way, and you are standing there, and say nothing, it could be cause for a disagreement. But the fallen nature in Eve was still independent and did not obey the will of God. I believe Adam was trying his best to make his wife comfortable and happy by recreating a replica of the Garden of Eden with the seeds God had given him. But something wasn't quite right. The Garden of Eden had perfect temperature, and it was so beautiful and breathtaking that God didn't even clothe them. As time began to change and Eve felt the chill from the turning of the seasons, and humidity from the heat, and the scent of the earth was not as pleasant. There were bugs and creeping things that were not so close in the Garden of Eden that were now vividly close. Eve's idea was to return to the Garden of Eden, where she was comfortable, and everything was at her reach. For the second thing, she had the seed, Abel, and, three, the promise given her that her seed would crush the serpent's head. Eve felt she didn't need any more children until she could fulfill the promise given her. I believe Eve would take the sheep and goats to feed in the pastures and would destroy every serpent or snake she could find, until Abel was of age to help her. She believed her son Abel was the promised seed and if she destroyed all the serpents, the Lord would remove the Cherubim who held the flaming swords and let her back into the garden. But because of Eve's choice to return to the garden, she neglected her husband in her passion to redeem herself from guilt and disobedience, so she could justify herself and be in good standing with the Lord and be restored from the damage she caused. During this time, the patience of Adam was being tested, and both sons were bringing offerings to the Lord to get answers. Cain brought the first fruits from the ground, and Abel brought the firstlings of his flocks, and the

Lord accepted Abel's offering, and answered by fire, but refused Cain's. Abel realized how the Lord sacrificed an innocent animal's life to pay for the cost of disobedience. Cain, feeling rejected by the Lord and jealous of Abel, slew him. Now Eve had no seed and Cain was forced to leave for killing his brother. Eve first lost her spiritual life with God and her husband and now two sons and was devastated. But if one would keep reading, we find Eve in a fight to overcome the fallen nature of the woman and become a woman of life. After Eve went through her time of grieving over her children and the decisions she made, she repented and obeyed the commands of God to be fruitful and multiply and to replenish the earth. She returned to her husband and fulfilled God's plan, so that life could be regenerated and the promise kept alive. Eve shows us that no matter how bad the mistakes we've made or the death of our loved ones, we can recover, forgive ourselves, and fight to move forward because the image of God was still in her and all she had to do was obey. She began to overcome every obstacle and leave behind the thought to be her own god. She set the narrative for the women in the generations to come, to keep the promise alive, by bearing children, waiting for her redeemer.

Chapter 5

Women of Life

As time passes, we find other women, like Sarah, Abraham's wife, who was barren and unable to have children. The Lord promised Abraham he would give him a seed, and his wife would conceive and birth a son. "Now Abraham and Sarah were old and well stricken in age; and it ceased to be with Sarah after the manner of women" (Genesis 18:11 KJV). At first Sarah didn't believe she could conceive in her old age, but through faith Sarah herself received strength to conceive and was delivered of a child when she was past age, and because she judged Him faithful who had promised. Sarah became a woman of life and believed the promise of God and kept alive the hope of a redeemer. These women of life would keep this promise of a redeemer alive, believing they may be the one to bring Him forth. Once the patriarchs began to form, the Israelites were about seventy people, and went to Egypt because of a famine, and became slaves for four hundred years. During this time, we discover the female image of God as a protecting weapon during the birth of Moses. In Exodus 1:16, it describes how the king of Egypt spoke to the midwives to kill the Hebrew sons, but to keep the daughters alive. But the midwives feared God and did not as the king of Egypt commanded them but saved the male children alive. If the men could not protect the women, then the women would protect the male children from being killed. Because the seed is in the male children, they carry the hope of a Savior. The shielding of life operates in the female image of God as a weapon against even the highest authority in the earth. "When Pharaoh enquired about why the midwives did not obey his orders to slay their sons. The midwives said unto Pharaoh, Because the Hebrew women are not like the Egyptian women; for they are lively and give birth before the midwives come in unto them" (Exodus 1:19 KJV). The king, being a man, couldn't contend with the nature of life in women, so he ordered his army to slay the children. All women have the ability to use their God-given power to stop evil men from destroying a race of people. We shall discover this in the coming pages of the Bible where women operated in the female image of God to preserve life. Moses' mother saw that Moses was a goodly child and hid him three months from Pharaoh's army, who was sent to kill all the Hebrew children two years and under. She trusted the Lord God as she put Moses in an ark and released him in God's care and protection, when she no longer could hide him. Pharaoh's daughter became a woman of life; she drew the child from the water, and called his name "Moses," and he became her son, and was in Pharaoh's house, the king who gave the command to kill all the male children. The next woman who operated in the female image of God was Deborah, a prophetess, a judge, and the wife of Lapidoth. she judged Israel at that time, and Deborah gave instructions to Barak, a military man, to defeat a strong Canaan

King named Jabin, who held the children of Israel captive for twenty years, according to the Book of Judges Chapter 4 (KJV). She called for Barak to gather an army to fight and free the Israelites as the Lord had given her directions. Barak followed her instructions and defeated King Jabin. Deborah in chapter 5:7 proclaimed that she arose as a mother in Israel, fulfilling the female image of God to help protect the children of Israel alive.

Chapter 6

Two Kinds of Women

Now God begins to reveal the difference between the two kinds of women. It has nothing to do with status, money, or position; it's the nature of the women. In the Bible, it shows the true choices that these two women make and how they stand by their decision. The first is two queens, during the reign of King Ahasuerus known as Xerxes, during the time of 486–465 B.C. This great king reigned from India even to Ethiopia, over one hundred and twenty provinces. During the first three years of his reign, he made a feast for his princes and servants. Queen Vashi, his wife, made a feast for the wives of the princes and servants, in the King's house. After a week, when the heart of the King was merry with wine. He sent his seven chamberlains that served in his presence to bring the queen before the King with the crown royal, to show the people and the princes her beauty, for she was fair to look on. But the queen Vashti refused to come at the King's command, by his chamberlains. This made the King furious, and he burned with anger. Most people may not understand the way a kingdom is operated, since we live in a democracy. This states where the word of a king is, there is power. In Ecclesiastes 8:4 (NKJV) it says, "And who may say unto him, 'What are you doing?'" No one can resist or question it. The King was supreme in his domain and he possessed absolute authority. Proverbs 20:2 states, "The fear of a king is as the roaring of a lion: whoso provoketh him to anger sinneth against his own soul." This is what Vashti the queen did before all the people in the kingdom toward her husband the King. Then the King said to the wise men concerning the law and judgment, "What shall we do unto queen Vashti according to the law?" Esther 1:15 KJV. One of the princes answered the king and said that Vashti the queen had not done wrong to the king only, by not obeying his command, but also to all the princes and the people in all the provinces of the king Ahasuerus. Because it was her husband the king, in his court, it would come abroad to all women and they would despise their husbands as well. Then the wise men spoke to the king to send out a royal decree and written among the laws of the Persians and Medes, and that it be not altered, to give her royal estate to another who was better. The degree stated that all wives shall give to their husbands, honor, both great and small. The letter was sent to every language and people throughout the provinces, that every man should bear rule in his own house. Here we find that even though this King of the Persians and Medes was not Jewish, it shows the authority built in all men, and that they uphold it and take it most seriously. Therefore, Vashti lost her crown, which represented reverence toward her husband, whether he was King or not. In the New Testament, the Apostle Paul in Ephesians 5:33 said, "Nevertheless let every one of you in particular so love his wife even as himself; and the wife see that she reverence her husband." This order was set in motion even in the garden with Adam and Eve in Genesis 3:16: "...and thy desire shall be to thy husband, and he shall rule over thee." This divine law is about the image of God, that he rules over his female nature and sets in order his divine operation for a man and a woman in marriage. This move by Vashti was motivated by a host of women in the feast during the celebration of King Ahasuerus, to plead to queen Vashti concerning their husbands. These wives of the princes did not have the scriptures that the Jewish women had and understood, and it cost queen Vashti her crown. The second queen brought to the King and because of her Jewish culture, displayed the unseen crown that some women wear, and are called women of life.

Queen Esther was chosen by King Ahasuerus, not only because she was beautiful, but what he was looking for, honor and respect, which Queen Esther displayed in his presence. In chapter 2:17, "And the king loved Esther above all the women, and she obtained grace and favor in his sight more than all the virgins…." The king's servants ministered to him to search for young virgins in all his provinces and gather them together that he may choose a new queen. So the king set the royal crown upon her head and made her queen instead of Vashti. Queen Esther had such reverence for her husband the king, that when the Jewish nation was about to be exterminated, because of a long history of an enemy close to the king. She hesitated to go before the king, because of the law, that no one could enter the king's court unless he, the king held out the golden scepter. Esther, the queen, put on her royal apparel and entered the king's court, and standing there, she obtained favor in his sight. The king held out the royal scepter to Esther, but Queen Esther made a bold statement, saying "… and if I perish, I perish" Esther 4:16 KJV. Because she could be banished like queen Vashti. In doing so, Queen Esther saved the whole nation of Israel from being annihilated, and she became a woman of life and protected the promise that a redeemer would come. The scriptures also give us two types of women in the next sequence during the reign of King Solomon. Two harlots (prostitutes) brought forth a case before King Solomon 1 Kings 3:16 (KJV). Then came two harlots to King Solomon and stood before him. (I'm going to condense the story). The first woman said that she and the other woman lived together in a house and each had a child; the other woman's child was three days after hers. And only those two were in the house. She continued to say the woman's child died in the night because she overlaid it, and arose at midnight and exchanged the dead child, and took her living child. When she rose in the morning to nurse her child, she saw it was dead, then she knew it was not her son. But the other woman said, "No the living is my son, and the dead is your son," and the first woman said, "No, the dead son is yours and the living is my son." Then the king rehearsed the sayings of both and said, "Bring me a sword," and they brought the king a sword. And the king said, "Divide the living child in two, and give half to the one, and half to the other." But the woman whose child was alive said to the king, for her bowels yearned for her son, "Give her the child and slay it not." But the other said, "Let it be neither mine nor hers but divide it." Then the king said, "Give her the living child, and slay it not, for she is the mother." Here we see clearly the woman of life and the woman of death. The woman of life tends to life and the woman of death tends to death, even though at any time the woman of death can choose life. The Bible always has two types of women, and no two are alike. In the book of Ruth, we find two sisters-in-law married to two brothers. One is Ruth, whom the book is written about and the other is Orpah, they were women of Moab, and their husbands were from Bethlehem-Judah. The mother-in-law was Naomi, and her husband and both sons died in the land of Moab. They left Bethlehem-Judah because of a famine. They dwelled in Moab for ten years, until she heard in the country of Moab how the Lord had visited his people in giving them bread. Naomi arose with her daughters-in-law, to return to her own country, in the land of Judah. Naomi spoke to her two daughters-in-law, to return to their own mothers' houses, and prayed for them to find husbands. Then she kissed them and wept with them because they stayed with her after their husbands had died. Now Naomi, while trying to say goodbye and to start her journey back to her land, but both Ruth and Orpah desired to return with Naomi to Bethlehem-Judah. Naomi tried to persuade both to turn back and go to their own people. As they kissed and wept again, Orpah gave her last affection and returned to her people and to her gods, but Ruth clave to her mother-in-law. She said, "Intreat me not to leave thee, or to return from following after thee: for whither thou goest, I will go; and where thou lodgest, I will lodge: thy people shall be my people, and thy God my God" Ruth 1:16 KJV. Ruth chose life, because the God of the Jews is Life. Orpah returned to Moab and their gods, but that was not a god of life. The female image of God is life. She's called life in the book of Proverbs, which we shall discover in person. Before that, in the book of Job, we find him asking about wisdom, because if one doesn't ask for this knowledge of wisdom which is with God, how can one comprehend her nature? In Job Chapter 28:12–13 Job asks the question, "But where shall wisdom be found, and where is the place of understanding? Man knoweth not the price thereof; neither is it found in the land of the living" (KJV). This Wisdom Job is asking about is not the earthly kind; it's only found in God. And unto man he said, "Behold the fear of the Lord, that is wisdom; and to depart from evil is understanding" Job 28:28 KJV. Job got the answer about wisdom, and that it fears or reverence the Lord and authority.

Chapter 7
Taught Wisdom

In the book of Proverbs, we find a king teaching his son, a prince, about the female image of God, and how to get the knowledge of wisdom and understanding. This famous king, whose name is King David, is the beloved psalmist and second king of Israel. He is introduced by his son, King Solomon, as to how his father taught him to pursue knowledge rightly and justly and what was required to achieve that goal. In 2 Chronicles 1:7, it says, "In that night did God appear unto Solomon, and said unto him, ask what I shall give thee" (KJV). In verse ten, Solomon said, "Give me now wisdom and knowledge, that I may go out and come in before this people: for who can judge this thy people, that is so great?" (KJV) King David must have rehearsed often to young Solomon about wisdom and understanding, that it was in his heart, even in his sleep. In 1 Kings 3:15 it says, "And Solomon awoke; and, behold, it was a dream" (KJV). The book of Proverbs is written mostly by King Solomon. The major theme that the king is addressing is about the female image of God which is the woman of life and the woman of death. The king had seven hundred wives and three hundred concubines, and for what purpose? To discover the lost name of women that was never known since the garden of Eden, when the woman fell in sin with no personal or spiritual name. Her true identity was unknown. King Solomon married women of all races and of different customs, so he could study their beliefs and teach them knowledge of their spiritual identity, but he found them unable to comprehend his teaching on the subject. In Ecclesiastes 7:28, Solomon came to this conclusion, "Which yet my soul seeketh, but I find not: one man among a thousand have I found; but a woman among all those have I not found" (KJV). In this statement, Solomon knew it was difficult to change a woman's identity and for them to accept their spiritual nature, being unfamiliar with the nature of God inside them. In the book of Proverbs, King Solomon began to tell us the female name in God that was hidden from most women and men.

Chapter 8
Wisdom is a Female Person

In Proverbs Chapter 7:4, it says, "Say unto wisdom, Thou art my sister; and call understanding thy kinswoman" KJV. Solomon calls wisdom a female, and he begins to introduce her in feminine form, as she speaks for herself. Chapter 8, Verse 12, it says, "I wisdom dwell with prudence, and find out knowledge of witty inventions" (KJV). In verses 14–15, "Counsel is mine, and sound wisdom; I am understanding. I have strength, by me kings reign, and princes decree justice" (KJV). And wisdom gives her credentials, she proclaims, "The Lord possessed me in the beginning of His way, before His works of old. I was set up from everlasting, from the beginning, or ever the earth was" Proverbs 8:22–23 KJV. Wisdom has much more to say about being a part of creation. Most religious people believe Jesus is wisdom, and he is. It's just that Jesus is male and female like his father, the almighty God. Wisdom says in the same chapter, "For whoso findeth me findeth life [eternal life], and shall obtain favor of the Lord" Proverbs 8:35 KJV. She is the eternal life that Jesus possesses and protects. She was so hidden that no angel knew she existed. For she states, "The Lord set her up from everlasting or ever the earth was to prove Wisdom is a part of creation." In Proverbs 8:24–25, she says, "When there were no depths, I was brought forth; when there were no fountains abounding with water, before the mountains were settled, before the hills was I brought forth…." "Then I was by him, as one brought up with him: and I was daily his delight, rejoicing always before him…." Proverbs 8:30 KJV. She has her own personality and was with Jesus in the creation of the Earth. But Solomon came upon another wisdom, and she was female also, this is when the Lord showed me through the writings of Solomon that there were two female spirits operating unseen in the earth. Solomon discovered this spirit by being married to so many women, because one cannot know the true nature of a woman except through marriage. The king studied his subjects' marriages as well and noticed a lot of men as far he could see on their rooftops at odd times of the night and day and wrote, "It is better to dwell in a corner of the housetop, than with a brawling woman in a wide house" Proverbs 21:9 and 25:24 KJV). As he studied the nature of the women, Solomon wrote what he saw as two different types of women that operated almost the same, but with a different spirit, and what caused these wives to be brawlers. As Solomon studied women, he saw one was of life, and the other of death. In chapter 7:6, the king saw through his window young men hanging out late at night and one woman dressed as a harlot approaches one man who went walking toward her house. She seduces him to come into her house, while her husband is away, and he does not know that it's for his life. "For she hath cast down many wounded: yea, many strong men have been slain by her" Proverbs 7:26 KJV. Remember wisdom's nature is she's a weapon, to give life or take it. "Her house is the way to hell, going down to the chambers of death" Proverbs 7:27 KJV. The wisdom that is life, she stands on the top of high places, by the way in the places of the path. There is a path to her, and it is through the knowledge of God's ways. She calls to people passing by to teach them life and to understand her ways. Because there is another wisdom also calling men. In chapter 9 of Proverbs, we see the two clearly. Wisdom builds her house, meaning her husband and children are built up by her grace and meekness. She hews out her seven pillars, her house is stable, because she lays out reverence, knowledge, understanding, purity, obedience, love, and peace, as its foundation. She prepared her food and mingled her wine, so no one would be over intoxicated. She sends forth her maidens into the streets, but she cries upon the highest places of the city, using radio or television, or any other medium. She says whoever is simple, let him turn in here, so as to give understanding of who she is. To dine with her, to eat her bread of knowledge and understanding. This wisdom is calling men and women, boys and girls, to protect them from the other wisdom that's calling them also. In Proverbs 9:13–18, Solomon describes the other wisdom as a foolish woman. She is clamorous, or loud, seductive, and unruly. She knows nothing about true wisdom. She tries to imitate true wisdom. "For she sitteth at the door of her house, on a seat in the high places of the city, to call passengers who pass by. She says whoever is simple come here, and for those that want understanding, she says to them, stolen waters are sweet, and bread eaten in secret is pleasant. But he knoweth not that the dead are there; and that her guests are in the depths of hell" KJV. Solomon noted there were two types of women, but also two types of female spirits. His understanding was so revealing that he knew to marry as many women as possible because of the nature in each one, and the powers they possessed. Solomon knew the dangers of them, because of the way they handled language. He could stop kings of other nations, because he married many of their daughters. This caused peace between his kingdom and theirs. The weapon that women are can stop one bullet, arrow, bomb, or war from being fired, because they were designed in the image of God to bring peace, and to prolong life. But if the woman is captured, she can be used as a weapon for strife and destruction. One can have wisdom whether poor or rich, but the Lord gives wisdom to kings, to teach them to rule in the fear of the Lord, and to learn justice, judgment, and equity (fairness). Wisdom is the female side of God, the Father. In Proverbs 4, the chapter shows King David explaining to his son Prince Solomon how to exalt and respect the female nature of God, and that she would give to his head an ornament of grace, and "a crown of glory shall she deliver" to him. Wisdom teaches her children to rule justly under the authority of the Lord. She teaches her children to avoid evil ways and protect themselves from choosing the wrong friends. Solomon writes, "It is the glory of God to conceal a thing, but the honor of kings is to search out a matter" Proverbs 25:2 KJV. The matter is the Spirit has King Solomon write how a man and woman should marry in the Lord. Proverbs 18:22 states that whoever finds a wife, finds a good thing and obtains favor of the Lord. And the connecting verse in Proverbs 19:14, "House and riches are the inheritance of fathers: and a prudent wife is from the Lord" KJV. It takes two witnesses to make a subject to be true. King Solomon is an earthly king representing a heavenly King, that's the purpose of King Solomon marrying so many wives. All born-again women are to be married to the Lord, first, after that a man. Only then can a man find her and obtain favor from the Lord. Many women are single because they're not married to Jesus, who is greater than Solomon. Wisdom is made out of treasure. King Solomon says, "She is more precious than rubies: and all the things thou canst desire are not to be compared unto her. Length of days is in her right hand and in her left hand, riches and honor. Her ways are ways of pleasantness, and all her paths are peace" Proverbs 3:15–17 KJV. This female spirit is made of spiritual jewels, rubies, diamonds, precious stones. In the last Chapter of Proverbs 31, King Solomon's mother is speaking to her son in using a nickname by calling him Lemuel, even though scholars are not sure whether this is King Solomon or another king. It appears King Solomon didn't know everything there is to know about women. His mother being female is teaching him the depths of a woman that he can't perceive. I believe the best one to teach King Solomon about natural women is his mother. Remember Bathsheba committed adultery with his father King David. At that time

Bathsheba, was a woman of death. Her husband was killed because of her, and the child she birthed died. She is teaching King Solomon there is hope for any woman who repents and chooses life. In the same chapter, she says, "Who can find a virtuous woman? Her price is far above rubies" Proverbs 31:10 KJV. If King David can teach his son Solomon about a spiritual female and her nature, should not his mother teach him about natural women, and their fallen nature and how to find the virtue in them? During the times of the kings, in Israel, there arose Queen Jezebel, who had killed some of the prophets of the Lord. This queen ruled Israel instead of her husband and made a decision to declare war against God's spokesman to his people. None of the men around her could be men. They were made eunuchs but hated her. So when Jehu, whom Elijah anointed to be king, came to withstand her, he looked up to see the eunuchs and asked if they were on his side, and said "Throw her down" 2 Kings 9:33 KJV. They threw her down and she hit the wall and horses and Jehu rode over her also with his horse. This female spirit is so dangerous that God Himself had to have a king contest this spirit operating in Queen Jezebel. But where does this female spirit originate from? And why does she fight against the authority God put in men?

Chapter 9

Wisdoms Identity

In Ezekiel Chapter 28, Verse 12 thru 19, we find the source of where this spirit comes from and who she's attached to. The Lord is commanding Ezekiel to take up a lamentation upon the king of Tyrus saying, "You seal up the sum, full of wisdom and perfect in beauty. You were in Eden, the garden of God; every precious stone was your covering" Ezekiel 28:13 NKJV. He continued by saying, "That he was perfect in the day he was created. First the Lord God has Ezekiel address an earthly prince of Tyrus, who set himself up to be a god, and to speak to him and pronounce his coming end and prove that a man will slay him. But the king of Tyrus is of a different nature and is higher than the prince." This judgment is against a fallen angel. In verse 14, he says, "You were the anointed cherub who covers: and I set you, so that you were upon the holy mountain of God; you have walked up and down in the midst of the stones of fire" KJV. But his heart was lifted up because of his beauty, and corrupted his wisdom, by reason of his brightness. As we can see, this anointed cherub, this heavenly being was at the very top of God's created beings, and God said he was perfect in all his ways. In order to be perfect, one would have to be male and female, holy and pure. In the book of Isaiah, God asks the question, "How art thou fallen from heaven, O Lucifer, son of the morning! How art thou cut down to the ground, which didst weaken the nations!" Isaiah 14:12 KJV. Here we find an angelic being whom God had made perfect, and full of wisdom and beauty, but he lifted up himself because of his brightness and perfection of his nature. Look closely and you will see God made him male and female, unlike God who is two thirds male and one third female. God created him half male and half female and determined the male side should rule his female side to keep the balance of power within himself. Even so the Lord put within this cherub two names, because of his dual nature. In the name Lucifer, is also Luci, because this a perfect being. Lucifer or Satan, as he's known, can change his shape and become a female or male at any time. This fight we're in is not against a male angel only but also a female; the name of his female side is wisdom also. King Solomon said that wisdom is better than weapons of war Ecclesiates 9:18. So the devil fights us with his weapon of wisdom. This fallen angel doesn't fight us physically, but with mind games, bad thoughts, offenses, and unforgiveness, in the hearts of men and women.

Chapter 10

Jesus brings Wisdom

In the New Testament we find two women of life about to change history. First God sends Gabriel the messenger angel to Bethlehem, to a high priest named Zechariah (Zacharias). The angel announced to him that God heard his prayers and he would be father to a son, even though he and his wife were very old. His wife Elizabeth became pregnant. Then the angel Gabriel went to a young woman to announce she was highly favored and would give birth to the Son of God. These two women miraculously birth sons in an unusual way than the norm. First Elizabeth is the wife of a high priest and walked with her husband perfectly before God, keeping his laws and commandments, but was past childbearing years as an old woman. We find these two women chosen by God who were still looking for the redeemer, that Eve herself began the process of obeying God and becoming a woman of life. But Mary is a young virgin, betrothed to Joseph, but the marriage is not yet consummated. Still believing God's messenger, that she was the one to fulfil the promise given. It's important how these two sons were born and how they grew. In the book of Luke, we see the difference between John the Baptist's growth and Jesus. In Luke 1:80, we see John the Baptist, "And the child grew, and waxed strong in spirit, and was in the deserts till the day of his shewing unto

Israel" KJV. In Luke 2:40, we see Jesus, "And the child grew, and waxed strong in spirit, filled with wisdom: and the grace of God was upon him." The difference between John and Jesus is Jesus was filled with wisdom, because he's the Son of God, and he's male and female. Both brought to earth something new that never existed before. No one had ever been born of the Spirit, like John and Jesus. Because Adam and Eve were created, not born. Jesus grew and increased in wisdom and stature and in favor with God and man. Jesus is not only the Son of God, but a man, and filled with wisdom the full image of God on earth. Jesus explained that he received this wisdom from his father. In John 5:26, "For as the Father hath life in himself; so hath he given to the Son to have life in himself" KJV. This life is wisdom, the same Wisdom as a female proclaimed in Proverbs 8:22, "The Lord possessed me in the beginning of his way, before his works of old" KJV. In order for any being to be God, he must be male and female, one whole person, not separated. As the Father gave Jesus this life in eternity past. He also gave him wisdom, the eternal life on earth. In John 1:4, he describes Jesus as having life in himself, "In him was life; and life was the light of men" KJV. This life that Jesus came to give us is the power over darkness, and to rule in his image, which is Light. Now Mary is a woman of life, and Jesus' earthly mother, but Mary is not born again. During the wedding that Jesus and his disciples were invited to, his mother was also there. "And when they wanted wine, the mother of Jesus saith unto him, they have no wine. Jesus saith unto her,

Woman, what have I to do with thee? Mine hour is not yet come" John 2:3–4 KJV. Jesus addresses her as a woman, and not as his mother. Jesus had to address Mary again, during one of his teaching sessions while Mary and his siblings were outside the meeting asking for him. Mark's Gospel Chapter 3, Verse 33-35 says, "And he answered them, saying, who is my mother, or my brethren?...For whosoever shall do the will of God, the same is my brother, and my sister, and my mother." Mary was operating in the fallen nature of the woman and was trying to control the man in Jesus. But in order to protect her, he had to put Mary, his mother aside, because she was under the influence of another wisdom. As Jesus was correcting the Pharisees concerning John the Baptist and how they rejected the counsel of God, to be baptized, He showed how they judged both him and John and said, "Wisdom is justified of her children" Luke 7:35 and Matthew 11:19 KJV. Wisdom is called a mother by Jesus and her two children on the earth are John the Baptist and Jesus. If the Son of God calls Wisdom a mother, how can we argue against him? This proves that she is female, for in the mouths of two or three witnesses, let every word be established. If Mary, Jesus' mother, had heard his teachings on the things of the spirit, she would have understood Jesus' actions toward her a little better. In John 3:6, Jesus brings all of us to the place where we partake of the same blessing as he and John the Baptist. To be born again is to go from our fallen nature to a new spiritual nature. Nicodemus, a Pharisee and a ruler of the Jews, came by night to discuss with Jesus his unusual way of teaching. Jesus answered him and said, "That which is born of the flesh is flesh, and that which is born of the Spirit is spirit" John 3:6 KJV. No one was ever born of the Spirit, except John the Baptist and Jesus. This is something new Jesus brought to the world. He expounded on this teaching so that we all can be redeemed back to the image of God. In chapter four he explained to a woman at the well that God is a Spirit and that we must worship God in spirit and in truth. One's spirit must be born again, so they can enter into the world of God which is Spirit. This is our true nature and it was lost in the Garden of Eden, by our first parents. While becoming independent from God's Spirit, their spirits died. Like fish out of water, mankind needs to live in the Spirit of God the way He designed us to live. As women have the power over death in childbearing, because of the female image of God in them, so does Jesus also have the power over death because he carried the male and female image of God in His Spirit. Jesus told Martha that He was the resurrection and the life in John 11:25 KJV. This power Jesus demonstrated multiple times in raising people from the dead. It's the female power that was in Eve, that she did not fully realize because of the fall. When we come to the cross, we find the Almighty God, the Father of Jesus, beginning to create a new man in Christ by first having His side pierced while in-between life and death. The same operation that was done in the first Adam, was done in the Last Adam to bring forth a new being born again. But before the new creation was brought forth, we find Mary, the mother of Jesus in the first book of Acts with the Apostles and others waiting for the baptism of the Holy Spirit to be born again. Because even though Mary gave birth to Jesus, she needed also to be born of the Spirit as John and Jesus were. We must all be born twice, first naturally, then spiritually.

Chapter 11

Paul's Teaching

The word "Woman" is mentioned many times in the Bible, and it's not always used in a good way. As we move forward to the epistles in the New Testament, we begin to understand why the Apostle Paul wrote concerning the fallen nature in women. There appears to be some confusion about women speaking or preaching in the pulpit or in church. Paul wrote in 1Timothy 2:11-12, "Let the women learn in silence with all subjection. But I suffer not from a woman to teach, nor to usurp authority over the man, but to be in silence." Paul is talking about the fallen nature of the woman, and the nature of God, according to the male and female order of function. In God's plural nature the female is under subjection to the male image of God for protection. Mainly because she is a divine weapon and can cause wars with her nature and words. If the female nature is out of order and operates over the male image, she becomes a spiritual weapon, out of control.

She can destroy everything around her while operating independently. Because her image is of God, the most powerful being in the universe. God never said he made the man in the image of a man, nor the woman in the image of a woman, but in His own image. Paul is dealing with the nature of women operating at home, where he's saying for them to learn to be in subjection to their own husbands. According to the image of God within them, so that the nature of God could be seen operating in the two, the way God functions in his image, as one. In 1 Corinthians 14:35 it says, "And if they will learn anything, let them ask their husbands at home: for it is a shame for a woman to speak in the church" KJV. The Apostle Paul is addressing the fallen nature of the born-again believers who were disrespectful toward their husbands at home, knowing it would spill over in the church. To teach the women or wives to learn their female image of God toward their own husbands, because they are both born again of the spirit. They need to learn the ways of the divine female spirit of God and to operate in her true identity. I remember in a church I attended, a woman said she believed Paul hated women, because he was not married. The confusion is still in the church over Paul's instructions concerning women and not to allow them to speak in church.

Paul also made another confusing statement, in Galatians 3:28: "There is neither Jew nor Greek, there is neither bond nor free, there is neither male nor female: for ye are all one in Christ Jesus." Notice how it's taken out of context, "neither male nor female." If you met a Jew, you can't tell him he's not a Jew, or a Greek, or any other ethnic group. This Epistle is written by a Jew, Paul; it's an eastern mind he's writing from, not a western mind.

In the East, the Jews have the Covenants, Laws, and Commandments and gave them to the world. The Jews are the nation of people God chose to bring these things of heaven to us and had them written for our learning. Paul is saying the Jews thought of themselves as the chosen people, over the Gentiles, which is every nation other than Israel. The ones who had freedom, thought of themselves as being above those who were slaves, and the males thought of themselves as being over all females. It can't be true, for there were queens in Paul's time as well as in King Solomon's time. The Jews were conquered by many nations in times past. In the Eastern regions, the male was given priority over the female in inheritance and the female was treated with much inequality, in almost everything. But in Christ all become equal, the female is equal with the male, because of the status of Christ who is above all ethnic groups or customs and laws. In Christ, the Jew is not above any Gentile, nor the slave below the freeman, for in Christ we are made a new creation. Ephesians 2:10 says, "For we are his workmanship, created in Christ Jesus unto good works, which God hath before ordained that we should walk in them." In this recreation of our spirits in Christ Jesus, a woman in Christ can be a preacher, teacher, but still not usurp authority over men; it still would be out of order. Paul made another powerful statement explaining who Christ is. "But unto them which are called, both Jews and Greeks [Gentiles], Christ the power of God, and the Wisdom of God" 1 Corinthians 1:24 KJV. Jesus the Messiah is carrying the Crown of wisdom, and her power, to combat a fallen angel, Lucifer, who is male and female. The female side of Lucifer is called wisdom also; we are fighting a devil that corrupted his wisdom, but he uses it against us, and sometimes, we don't know when he switches genders on us. In 1 Corinthians 2:6, Paul says "…we speak wisdom among them that are perfect [mature spiritually]: yet not the wisdom of this world, nor of the princes of this world…." KJV.

Chapter 12

Two Wisdoms

There are two wisdoms operating in this world by the speaking of life or death. In the book of James, we find the two wisdoms again, but much clearer in their operation. In the first chapter of James, we find in verse five, "If any of you lack wisdom, let him ask of God, that giveth to all men liberally, and upbraided not; and it shall be given him." One has to ask God for wisdom, because he is the only one that has this pure kind, and one must learn about the wisdom God gives to them. In verse 12, she's called the crown of life, to help us rule over our souls, and our enemies. As we increase in learning about the wisdom God gives, and not the wisdom of this world, we begin to grow and learn about the hidden wisdom, which is for our glory. In Chapter 3:14–18, "But if ye have bitter envy and strife in your hearts, glory not, and lie not against the truth. This wisdom descendeth not from above, but is earthly, sensual, devilish" KJV. James is saying this kind seems right, but is not from heaven and is engaged in bitterness, of arguing and strife, of unforgiveness never wanting to show mercy or forgive wrongs done to them. But the wisdom that is from above is first pure, then peaceable, gentle, and easy to be intreated (submissive) full of mercy and good fruits (deeds), without partiality, without hypocrisy. This wisdom shows no favors, and doesn't look for faults, but works with love to cover them, instead of exposing them to hurt or do harm. The two wisdoms operate contrary to each other and they can be at times difficult to divide because we all can operate in both at different times. The wisdom that's from above helps us to cut off the earthly wisdom we are accustomed to think and speak from. To eradicate the working of the earthly wisdom in our lives and to keep our crown of the heavenly wisdom, until we become fully mature. The wisdom from Lucifer is designed to seduce both men and women and to rule them and keep them in the dark from the knowledge of God's wisdom. Once women find their true spiritual identity in Christ, they will begin to dominate the earthly wisdom and teach this knowledge to girls and boys so they can know what they're fighting and how to win. It's not enough for a few people to have victory and it becomes a show and performance. Instead of everyone ruling and triumphant in Christ together helping each other in victory and fulfilment. The main ones left behind are the women whom the church is full of and faithful to.

Chapter 13
John's Revelation

In Revelation 1:6 it says, "And hath made us kings and priests unto God and His Father; to Him be glory and dominion for ever and ever Amen." In Christ, the women are made kings and priests unto God, as single women they are married to the Lord, and not to men, they are Kings, priests or preachers Revelation 5:10 KJV. But if born again women are married to the Lord and a man, she is a queen and a priest. We must understand in the new birth everyone is equal, but there is a hierarchy in the ranks. We are all under authority, some greater, some lesser. In Revelation 12:1 John wrote, "And there appeared a great wonder in heaven; a woman clothed with the sun, and the moon under her feet, and upon her head a crown of twelve stars" KJV. This symbol is a picture of the Church and the twelve tribes of Israel wearing the crown of Wisdom ruling over God's creative works. The other female spirit is like a great city where she sits. This same spirit as in Proverbs chapter 9, but in Revelation 17:3, "So he [the angel] carried me away in the spirit into the wilderness: and I saw a woman sit upon a scarlet colored beast, full of names of blasphemy, having seven heads and ten horns." The symbols of these two female spirits who were written to show one ruling in the heavens, and one ruling on earth. Remember Adam and the woman fell in the animal kingdom, and their spirits became like that of an animal, they still possessed the soul of a human being, but the spirit of an animal. People still look up their zodiac signs and believe the animal image they were born under. It's primarily in the schools, colleges and the sports world. In China, it's called the year of the dragon or some other animal name. That's why we must be born of God's spirit, to have human spirits again. This spirit in the woman desires to rule beastly men and does because the fallen female spirit of Lucifer desires to usurp authority over men until we are born again. God says things about the fallen nature of women, because in the natural world the women are protected by law from the beastly nature of men. In the kingdom of God, the reverse is true. God must protect men from the fallen nature in women until they come to marry the Lord and learn of their spiritual nature in

Him. In Revelation 14:4, it says, "These are they which were not defiled by women; for they are virgins…." KJV. The female image of God must be brought to the forefront and given her rights to function as the Holy Spirit leads. The changes we need will begin to take place in our homes, neighborhoods, workplace, churches and nation. The families will begin to flourish as husbands and wives return to the image of God and his order. The economy will spring forth in time. The young adults won't run wild in the street because stability will be in the home. When the female gets back to the image of God.

Without her help functioning in the female image of God, the body of Christ suffers, leaving her undeveloped remaining cheerleaders and chanting scriptures without understanding the meaning.

Until the women embrace their spiritual nature and join the Lord and her husband, in this spiritual fight, the casualties will increase. In the book of Revelation when Jesus is explaining to John who he is, Jesus says that He is the Alpha and Omega. The Alpha is the ruling male— the Beginning, and the Omega is the female—the Ending. In the beginning, man lived much longer than women, but in these last days the women will outlive the men, because they are the Omega of God. In the end, God is raising up His image in women to come forth and operate in Him and redeem the fallen nature of Eve from the beginning.

www.ingramcontent.com/pod-product-compliance
Lightning Source LLC
Chambersburg PA
CBHW071226160426
43196CB00012B/2421